The Harry Potter Cocktail Cookbook

35 Extraordinary Drink Recipes Inspired by The Wizarding World of Harry Potter

By Daisy Mellema

TABLE OF CONTENT

Introduction

Irresistible potions culled from one of the most excellent books of all times. The Harry Potter books contain some of the most magical sips that exist. Potion makers (bartenders) all across the world have confirmed that the subtle science and exact art of potion-making (that's "bartending," to Muggles) is complicated, but it can easily be mastered through apt practice and a natural flair for the art. Professor Severus Snape once said that a good potion can "bewitch the mind and ensnare the senses". Embedded in the chapters are cocktails that in his opinion can "bottle fame, brew glory, and even put a stopper in death," if you know what you're doing. Potion Making is a versatile type of magic, and the concoctions that are brewed are a clear example of this.

While purebloods can add a few magical enchantments to their potions, muggles, on the other hand, can stick to replicating these magical potions in the form of what they call "cocktails". Here are some irresistible sips that are bound to ignite your inner wizard and turn your occasion into a fun affair.

Chapter 1 Irresistible Wizard's Indulgence

Potion making goes beyond the natural ability possessed by witches. In these modern times, muggles refer to it as mixology. This exceptional talent is possessed only by witches and strong warlocks of the magical realm, some of which are Professor Severus Snape, Hermione Granger and Slughorn. It involves the art of elaborating liquids with magical properties so they can be used for a myriad of tasks, some of which include helping to strengthen a vast range of spells, recreating spells, producing magically induced effects on the consumer. But these aside, let's go straight to the point. Most potions are simply made to be enjoyed as mere drinks. To this, we are interested to include and wish to explore.

The irresistible wizards' indulgence is a compilation of cocktails inspired by famous witches and wizards in the Harry Potter franchise. In the most simplistic sense, these cocktails are magical mixtures, but for the muggles trying out the recipes within this book, these are made out of ordinary ingredients. They can be most certainly made by a person without magical qualities. However, just like everything perfect, they require continuous practice and strict abidance to the instructions in order to capture the essence of the wizard that inspired them. Within this chapter contain delicious sips from famous wizards and witches.

Witch's Blood Brew Cocktail

Not your regular mixed fruit cocktail, the Witch's Blood Brew Cocktail is a drip off the hallowed essence of Harry Potter witch favourite. It embodies all the sweet but scary memories of the book we've all come to over. Just a sip and you're hexed on to it. The cocktail is a Harry Potter original culled from Harry Potter yule dance scene in the goblet of fire. Who didn't want a sip when Hermione took one after her dance with Viktor Krum?

The delicious sip off blood-like rimmed goblet is made with Himalayan salt, blood syrup, mixed juices (orange, lime, cherry, pomegranate), and vodka, good thing most of these are available ingredients hence, there's no need porking to the Diagon Alley. The drink has a sweet-tart-salt like the taste. If you're a fan of all things vodka-based, then this is the right drink for you. This recipe is perfect for a big party as it's so easily doubled/tripled, and you can make them for kids without any vodka.

This Witch's Blood Harry Potter Cocktail is perfect for whipping up delicious sips in a big batch for a crowd. An easy way to make a cocktail that mixes vodka, whiskey, and lemon together to create a twist on a sour whiskey recipe, but with the added sweetness of the cherry.

Let's quickly take a look at how this enchanted sip is made.

Prep time: 10 muggle minutes
Serves: 4

Ingredients
- ¼ cup tart cherry juice
- ¼ cup orange juice
- ½ teaspoon fresh ginger
- 3 teaspoons lime juice
- ¼ sparkling water or soda
- 3.5 ounces red gel color + corn syrup – for blood-stained rims
- 1.5 ounces black sugar + himalayan salt
- Dry ice – optional

Instructions
1. Prepare and rim the glasses with blood syrup. To get this done, prepare the corn syrup and red gel colour, rim the glasses, and put in a fridge to set.
2. Cast all juices, ginger, regular ice and vodka into a large jar.
3. Close up the lid and shake the mixture vigorously to combine.
4. Take out already set and rimmed glasses from the fridge and pour in strained juice-vodka in all glasses. Stop halfway through.
5. Add sparkling water.
6. Add dry ice.
7. Stir in and serve.

Note: always be extra cautious when using dry ice as it can quickly burn your fingers on contact or any body part if touched. Always ensure the dry ice effect wears out or melts before sipping the cocktail. It just gives it the witchy effect hence can be skipped.

Nutrition Facts per Serving
Calories 0, Total Fat 0g, Saturated Fat 0g, Total Carbs 0g, Net Carbs 12g, Protein 0g, Sugar 45g, Fiber 0g, Sodium 0g, Potassium 0g

Wizard's Brew Cocktail

Wizard's Brew is a wizarding brand of sweet stout (Stout is a dark, top-fermented beer with a number of variations, including dry stout, Baltic porter, milk stout, and imperial stout.) sold in wizarding pubs, such as the Leaky Cauldron, the Fountain of Fair Fortune, and The Hopping Pot, all in Diagon Alley, London. Wizard's Brew is presumably derived from "witch's brew," a term for a concoction of strange ingredients. This punch is a homage to the Hogwart's fierce spirit. It can be made ahead of time in big batches, freeing you up to mingle with the other witches... er, we mean guests. Made of orange juice, pomegranate juice and citrus vodka, it goes down.

This unique cocktail originated in London, England, in the early 1720s. Witches and wizards will love this magic brew, all thanks to its thick sweet flavor. Without more ado, pull out your cauldron to scare up a batch of this party-perfect wizard punch. This recipe is quite simple and can be adjusted for any size crowd. Two parts orange juice, two parts pomegranate juice, and one part citrus vodka. Stir or shake to combine and you're ready to party!

Prep time: 3 muggle minutes
Serves: 2

Ingredients
- 6 cups orange juice
- 6 cups pomegranate juice
- 3 cups citrus vodka

Notes
For a smaller batch:
- 2 parts orange juice
- 2 parts pomegranate juice
- 1 part vodka

Instructions
1. Pour in the orange juice, pomegranate juice, and vodka into a cocktail container of choice. I chose a 1-gallon glass jug.
2. Shake or stir to combine, and serve.
3. Refrigerate all portions of the unused cocktail in a sealed container for up to three days. It starts to taste strange after that.

Nutrition Facts per Serving
Calories 209, Total Fat 0g, Saturated Fat 0g, Total Carbs 23g, Net Carbs 0g, Protein 1g, Sugar 20g, Fiber 0g, Sodium 110g, Potassium 411g.

Severus Snape's Darkness

Leave it to the potions master to cook up the best potion (cocktails) the wizarding world has come to love. Inspired by Snape's indescribable love for all things dark and his unusual black ensemble, this cocktail is a herbaceous "elixir" like a sip that invokes the fantasy theme associated with the uncanny professor.

The Severus Snape cocktail was first recreated by a muggle mixologist M Simmons. Although this version came close to that which Snape first created, there is still more to add. The seven ingredient cocktail is a must-have for any Harry Potter themed party. After you're done making it, get into character in a stealth dark cape-like Professor Snape, but the spike of plentiful, flavorful amaretto might represent his hidden good qualities that are floating in the sea of darkness that is his soul. Here's how the Severus Snape is made.

Prep time: 5 muggle minutes
Serves: 2

Ingredients
- 1 rinse Absinthe
- ½ cup of ice
- 2 ounces Bourbon
- 1/4 ounce Averna
- 1/2 ounce sweet vermouth
- 1 tablespoon root liqueur
- 3 ds orange bitters

Instructions
1. Rinse the cocktail glass with absinthe and chill in the freezer for some time.
2. Stir in all the remaining ingredients over ice until chilled. Strain contents into a chilled and rinsed cocktail glass.
3. Spray a dash of absinthe onto the drink.

Nutrition Facts per Serving
Calories 2, Total Fat 0g, Saturated Fat 0g, Total Carbs 0g, Net Carbs 0g, Protein 0g, Sugar 0.3g, Fiber 0g, Sodium 50g, Potassium 0g

Witch's Heart Blackberry Cocktail

If you have a craving for all things mystic and ghostly, then the Witch's Heart Blackberry Cocktail is the right sip for you. Created by an unknown potion witch, this purple glass of mystery is amongst the oldest cocktails in the ministry of magic. It embodies everything ghostly and unseen. The beautiful purple color with the shimmery liquid just calls out to every Potterhead to come to take a sip.

The Witch's Heart Blackberry Cocktail is so simple to make, and you can adapt it to your taste absolutely any way you want. Also, like a blackberry based sip, it looks so gorgeous you could make this for any kind of themed party too. It looks so mesmerizing. This is the perfect witch's brew!

Prep time: 10 minutes
Serves: 2

Ingredients
- ½-2 teaspoon powdered dry ice
- 1 shot apple brandy
- ½ cup purple shimmery liqueur
- ½ cut blended ice cube
- 1 teaspoon grenadine syrup

Instructions
1. Add about 1/2 to 1 teaspoon of powdered dry ice to the bottom of a martini glass (optional).
2. Cast in the apple brandy and purple shimmery liqueur in a shaker.
3. Add 1 ice cube and shake for a few seconds to chill the drink. Strain the cocktail into a martini glass. Add in more purple shimmery liqueur if necessary, but it's advisable.
4. Pour in 1 teaspoon of grenadine syrup, about an inch from the surface of the drink – the grenadine should sink to the bottom, creating a "bleeding" effect.
5. Add about 1/2 teaspoon of powdered dry ice on top and serve with a stirrer, so that your guests can stir the "potion" to create that shimmery, smoky effect.

Note: This cocktail can be made with Purple Shimmery Liqueur and mix it with some White Moscato Wine.

Nutrition Facts per Serving
Calories 71, Total Fat 0g, Saturated Fat 0g, Total Carbs 0g, Net Carbs 0g, Protein 0g, Sugar 54g, Fiber 0g, Sodium 320g, Potassium 430g.

The Death Eater

A tribute to the villains we all love to hate. Every diehard Potterhead sure does despise the wicked minions Voldemort always sends out to do his evil bidding. Culled in the dark, gory smoke, they sprawled the magical realm causing mayhem and inflicting misery wherever they went. But, for whatever reservation we hold against them, one thing is certain. They sure know how to throw the best feasts and make the best cocktails.

It's no secret that most death eaters are Slytherin; thus, the characteristic green glow of the cocktail. Just like the trail of dark smoke they let off when they flee from a scene. The Harry Potter inspired Death Eater's cocktail shimmers green characteristic of most Slytherin villains. Made with blue curacao and Midori, it's absolutely delicious. Even Voldemort will be jealous.

The cocktail comes with a characteristic sweet-sour pineapple flavour. However, to throw you off the actual scent, there are traces of vodka, Blue Curaçao, and Midori. We can't help but admit that this is one tasty sip from the bad guys.

Prep time: 5 muggle minutes
Serves: 2

Ingredients
- 1 ounce vodka
- 1 ounce Blue Curacao
- 1/2 ounce Midori or other melon liqueur
- 1 ounce Sweet and Sour Mix
- 3 ounces pineapple juice
- 1 teaspoon silver cake shimmer
- Optional: Wilton Zombie Hands Candy for Peter Pettigrew's Hand
- Optional: Maraschino Cherry, for garnish

Instructions
1. Fill up a cocktail shaker with ice.
2. Cast in all ingredients in a cocktail mixer, shake thoroughly to combine.
3. Pour out the content into a cocktail glass.
4. Pour over the ice into a beverage glass.
5. Optional: you can top off with a zombie hand candy as peter Pettigrew's hand.
6. Sprawl around the party grudgingly like a real death eater and enjoy.

Nutrition Facts per Serving
Calories 219, Total Fat 0g, Saturated Fat 0g,
Total Carbs 0g, Net Carbs 0g, Protein 0g,
Sugar 56 g, Fiber 0g, Sodium 100g,
Potassium 0g.

The Albus Dumbledore

We all know the beardy professor had a sweet tooth. He was a sucker for all things sweet and fruity, so it's no secret there's a secret cocktail out there in his name. The Albus Dumbledore was coined from one of the headmaster's famous quotes and conversation with Professor McGonagall.

> **"Would you care for a lemon drop?"**
> **"A what?"**
> **"A lemon drop. They're a kind of Muggle sweet I'm rather fond of.**
> **— Albus Dumbledore to Minerva McGonagall**

Harry Potter and the Sorcerer's Stone

Inspired by the lemon drop candy, which the professor loved, the cocktail carries with it similar ingredients found in the sweet especially the signature ingredient lemon. Unlike other easy to make cocktails on the list, the Albus Dumbledore is a little complicated, well you don't expect a cocktail dedicated to the most powerful wizard to be a leisurely stroll. Let's take a look at how to conjure this up.

Prep time: 5 muggle minutes
Serves: 2

Ingredients
- 1 shot lemon-flavored vodka
- 2 ounces sprite
- 4 ounces coconut whipped cream (I found mine at Sprouts, but you can make it using recipes like this)
- ½ teaspoon lemon zest
- 2 ounces ice

Instructions
1. Cast ice into a glass.
2. Add 1-2 shots of lemon vodka, depending on what you like. Generally, lemon is preferred by many.
3. Proceed to fill up your drink the rest of the way with Sprite. Stir in all ingredients together.
4. Top up the glass with coconut whipped cream together.
5. Enjoy!

Note: if you're a sucker for Italian creme soda, you're definitely going to love this one. They taste just like. Unlike most cream-based cocktails, it is dairy-free, perfect if you're dairy intolerant.
Nutrition Facts per Serving

Nutrition Facts per Serving
Calories 60, Total Fat 0g, Saturated Fat 22g, Total Carbs 34g, Net Carbs 0g, Protein 6.2g, Sugar 51g, Fiber 0g, Sodium 0.2g, Potassium 0g.

Voldemort Dark Lord Cocktail

Gather round cocktail-loving wizards, though the dark lord is gone, his affluence hasn't dwindled one bit, and though we are as petrified about this cocktail as ever, rumours have it that it's an excellent mix. Make no mistakes, the delicious cocktail does not in any way honor the evil villain He-who-must-not-be-named, it earns its name as one of the deathliest cocktails on the list thanks to the jalapeno pepper.

This deathly and robust cocktail is a fearful blend of three potent ingredients, tequila, Tabasco sauce and jalapeno pepper. The tough cocktail, just like the dark lord, is known to knock even the most potent wizard off his feet. It's imperative to drink responsibly. Remember, it's named after Lord Voldemort for a reason! Please beware!

Prep time: 5 muggle minutes
Serves: 1

Ingredients
- 1-ounce tequila
- ½ ounce Tabasco sauce
- 1 jalapeno pepper

Instructions
1. Muddle jalapeno pepper and tobacco sauce.
2. Strain mixture into a shot glass.
3. Add tequila.
4. Garnish the cocktail with thin slices of jalapeno.

Nutrition Facts per Serving
Calories 70, Total Fat 0g, Saturated Fat 0g, Total Carbs 0g, Net Carbs 0g, Protein 0g, Sugar 54g, Fiber 0g, Sodium 0g, Potassium 0g

Witch's Brew Punch

When the students at Hogwarts want to go all out on their spooky side, the Witches' Brew Punch is their go-to potion. Embodying the gory and dreadful essence of witchcraft in yet a sweet delicious manner, the punch is a gorgeous, slightly repulsive, green colour, with chunks of melting sherbet that could gross out even the most delighted wizard when they scoop it.

So slimy yet delicious, the Witch's Brew Punch will undoubtedly make all your goblins grin! It's an easy sparkling lime punch the whole coven will love. Add in dry ice to the punch bowl for an extra spooky effect! This lime pineapple punch is a fun punch for a Harry Potter-themed Halloween, perfect when served in a festive bowl. But, also a great tasting punch you can make quickly and serve whenever you want, especially lovely in the summer heat.

You can lighten-up this punch recipe by using diet ginger ale or the lower-sugar version. Most potion makers always make the lightened-up version, and it's still a hit and turns out delicious.

Prep time: 5 minutes
Serves: 4 quarts

Ingredients
- 1-quart lime sherbet
- 1 (2-litre) ginger ale, chilled
- 1 block dry ice
- 1 (46-ounce) can unsweetened pineapple juice, chilled
- 1/4 cup freshly squeezed lime juice
- Large cauldron
- Punch bowl that fits inside a cauldron
- Optional: a few drops of green food colouring for added effect

Instructions
1. Let's start out with the dry ice. Break in the dry ice into large pieces using a mallet or other tool. Be careful that you use gloves when handling it since it can cause burns if it comes into contact with your skin. Place some of the dry ice in the bottom of your cauldron. Put the remaining dry ice in a cooler nearby. Pour some hot water on top of the ice so that it starts to smoke.
2. Place the punch bowl on top of the dry ice inside the cauldron. Cast in the ginger ale, pineapple juice, lemon juice, and any other juice into the punch bowl.
3. Stir continuously until they combine.
4. Scoop in lime sherbet, mix slightly for a while until sherbet starts to melt.
5. Top off with scarry looking spooky eyes (you can find these plastic eyeballs at Target, Michaels and most craft stores).
6. Tips: Orange Pineapple Punch is an excellent flavour for any time of year. Top punch bowl with mint leaves or fresh cut orange slices for a refreshing taste.
7. Other Cool Treats: Pour leftover punch into ice-cube trays and freeze. Flavoured ice-cubes can be chopped in a blender. Spoon mixture into ice-cream bowls. Serve immediately. Enjoy eating this new twist on orange creamsicle crush cool new frounceen treat!

Nutrition Facts per Serving
Calories 18, Total Fat 0g, Saturated Fat 0g, Total Carbs 41g, Net Carbs 0g, Protein 2g, Sugar 0g, Fiber 0g, Sodium 840g, Potassium 43g

Nearly Headless Nick Deathday Cocktail

Nicholas de Mimsy-Porpington known after his death as Nearly Headless Nick, (d. 31 October 1492) was a wizard who attended Hogwarts School of Witchcraft and Wizardry and was sorted into Gryffindor House. As the most famous ghost in the great hall and the official resident ghost of Gryffindor, Sir Nick, as he's fondly called by students, is the jolly good and friendly spirit little wonder why everyone was sad when he was petrified by the basilisk in chambers of secret.

The Nearly Headless Nick Deathday Cocktail was inspired by the mandrake potion administered to the friendly ghost when he was petrified by the scary basilisk. Although we can't get our hands on an actual mandrake, this cocktail recipe is as close as you can get it to the real potion administered to Sir Nick.

Honestly, the taste of Nearly Headless Nick Deathday Cocktail can be bone-chilling itself. Consider stirring the bold, herbal liqueur with dark rum and creamy coffee liqueur. The result is a creamy, balanced drink with notes of coffee grounds and ground roots. Here's how it's made.

Prep time: 5 muggle minutes
Serves: 2

Ingredients
- ✵ 1 ounce Mount Gay Rum
- ✵ 2 ounces Mr. Black Cold Brew Coffee Liqueur
- ✵ 1 ounce Jägermeister
- ✵ 2 dashes of Angostura Bitters
- ✵ Simple syrup – measure with stir spoon
- ✵ Glass: rocks

Instructions
1. Cast all ingredients in a cocktail bowl.
2. Stir well until they combine.
3. pour over a single ice cube in a rocks glass.
4. Nutrition Facts per Serving

Nutrition Facts per Serving
Calories 120, Total Fat 0g, Saturated Fat 0g, Total Carbs 54g, Net Carbs 0g, Protein 0g, Sugar 40g, Fiber 0g, Sodium 220g, Potassium 0g

The Grey Lady

Helena Ravenclaw, more commonly referred to as The Grey Lady, is the house ghost for Ravenclaw. She is the daughter of Rowena Ravenclaw. Before her death, the grey lady attended Hogwarts School of Witchcraft and Wizardry and was obviously sorted into Ravenclaw house. The grey lady is not mentioned much in the Harry Potter books, except in Harry Potter and the Deathly Hallows, where Harry needs to find out where the diadem of Ravenclaw is.

The Grey Lady cocktail pays tribute to the ghost of Helena Ravenclaw. Just like the peaceful spirit of Helena Ravenclaw, the primary ingredient of the cocktail the Plymouth Gin has a relatively neutral flavor profile and won't fight with the other ingredients in this drink. Indeed, an exciting fusion of tasty alcoholic relief in silver-grey essence.

Prep time: 5 minutes
Serves: 1

Ingredients

- 3/4 ounce Plymouth Gin
- 3/4 ounce Cocchi Americano
- 3/4 ounce St. Germain Elderflower Liqueur
- 3/4 ounce lemon juice
- 1 dash Peychaud's Bitters

Instructions

1. Cast all parts in a cocktail shaker filled with ice.
2. Shake vigorously.
3. Strain contents into a coupe or cocktail glass.
4. Serve chilled.
5. Nutrition Facts per Serving
6. Calories 143, Total Fat 0g, Saturated Fat 0g, Total Carbs 0g, Net Carbs 0g, Protein 0g, Sugar 43g, Fiber 0g, Sodium 0g, Potassium 0g

Nutrition Facts per Serving
Calories 143, Total Fat 0g, Saturated Fat 0g, Total Carbs 0g, Net Carbs 0g, Protein 0g, Sugar 43g, Fiber 0g, Sodium 0g, Potassium 0g

Moaning Myrtle Bubbly Vodka

Myrtle Warren, popularly known as moaning myrtle, is the ghost of a young female student killed on the second-floor girl's lavatory of Hogwarts castle. Ever since then, she's haunted the bathroom. Myrtle might be all hostile and grumpy to anyone who stepped into the bathroom but for Harry and his friends, she's ever ready to listen and divulge old secrets.

Inspired by the bubbly theme of Myrtle's drowning voice, the tasty ghostly cocktail may seem sweet at first sight, but never let its invisible exterior fool you. The fizzy flavor will sure sneak up on you when you least expect it. The good news is you don't have to hang out in the ladies' bathroom to find this martini, and you won't want to avoid it either. The bubbly champagne and vodka cocktail are lightly sweetened with white grape juice than a pretty purple sugar rim for the perfect ghostly touch.

Prep time: 5 muggle minutes
Serves: 1

Ingredients
- ✡ 2 ounces champagne
- ✡ 1 ounce vodka
- ✡ 2 ounces white grape juice
- ✡ Purple sugar
- ✡ Optional: dry ice

Instructions
1. Pour a small amount of grape juice onto a plate and a small amount of purple sugar on a different dish. Dip the rim of the glass in the juice and then in the sugar until the rim is coated.
2. Add vodka, white grape juice, and ice to a martini shaker and shake until chilled. Pour into the martini glass and add the chilled champagne.
3. For a ghostly effect, add a small piece of dry ice.

Nutrition Facts per Serving
Calories 50, Total Fat 0g, Saturated Fat 0g,
Total Carbs 0g, Net Carbs 0g, Protein 0g,
Sugar 12g, Fiber 0g, Sodium 0g, Potassium 0g

Ronald Weasley

R onald Weasley is Harry's best friend and confidant. The grumpy redhead has a cocktail dedicated to him as we look at some of the unique Harry Potter cocktails, especially this particular one inspired by Ron Weasley, Harry's right-hand man. This particular cocktail is a whole different ballgame and mixed up four distinct rious alcohols, so this is quite a potent cocktail.

Who wouldn't want to have a Ronald Weasley in their parties? Just like the character it embodies, it has a bit of everything. This particular recipe starts out with a little whiskey, then Campari (a bitter red Italian drink). It's a little rough and bitter due to Ron's fearless attitude. The Ron Weasley owes a little bit to the Old Pal, appropriately, and also a bit to the Blood and Sand in its essence, it is manly, strong, a bit sweet, and a little bitter.

Prep time: 5 muggle minutes
Serves: 2

Ingredients
- ☼ 1½ ounces rye whiskey
- ☼ ¾ ounce cherry brandy (I used cherry heering.)
- ☼ ½ ounce Campari
- ☼ ½ ounce sweet vermouth
- ☼ 1 ounce fresh-squeezed orange juice

Instructions
1. Cast all ingredients into a cocktail glass filled with ice.
2. Stir for thirty seconds.
3. Strain into the central cocktail glass for your drinking pleasure or allow to melt.
4. Garnish with cherries or lemon slices.

Nutrition Facts per Serving

Calories 76, Total Fat 0g, Saturated Fat 0g,
Total Carbs 0g, Net Carbs 0g, Protein 0g,
Sugar 80g, Fiber 0g, Sodium 332g, Potassium 0g

Filius Flitwick's Charmed Cherry Soda

Professor Filius Flitwick was a half-goblin wizard, the charms master as well as the Head of Ravenclaw House, being an intelligent young man and conscientious tutor. His cheery demeanor was also expressed in creativity. At Christmas, he delighted in making decorations, even enlisting live fairies into the festive fun. One of the hidden secrets about him is his subtle addiction to cherry sodas and potions.

In Harry Potter and The Prisoner of Azkaban: (Ch 10, p 202). Harry, who was not given permission to leave Hogwarts or go to the village, hides under a table at the Three Broomsticks public house. He is about to overhear the Minister of Magic explain that Sirius Black is Harry's godfather when Madame Rosmerta arrives with drinks for the Professors.

Flitwick's drink of choice is cherry syrup and soda with ice and an umbrella. Here is a fresh and straightforward cherry syrup recipe that can be paired with your choice of Setzer soda water, club soda, or even a cream soda if you want it sweet.

Harry Potter and The Prisoner of Azkaban: Ch 10, p 202.

Next, he saw another pair of feet, wearing sparkly turquoise high heels, and heard a woman's voice.
"A small gilly water—"
"Mine," said Professor McGonagall's voice.
"Four pints of mulled mead—"
"Ta, Rosmerta," said Hagrid.
"A cherry syrup and soda with ice and umbrella—"
"Mmm!" said Professor Flitwick, smacking his lips.

Inspired by Flitwick's love for cherry soda, here's a sweet cocktail close enough and an excellent replica to what the cherry professor had. This recipe contains an alcohol option for an adult version because let's face it—not all of us can put up with troublesome students as well as Professor Flitwick can. And remember, it's swish and flick!

Prep time: 1 hour
Serves: 2

Ingredients
- 2 cups frounceen or fresh black cherries
- 1/2 cup sugar
- 1/2 water
- Lemon juice
- Setzer Soda Water
- 1 shot plain vodka + 1 shot lemon-flavored vodka (optional)
- Ice

Instructions
1. To make the cherry syrup.
2. Cast in the fruit, sugar, water, and lemon juice into a medium pot over low heat and cook until sugar is dissolved.
3. Grind up the cherries against the side of the pot and set to boil over medium heat.
4. Stir and boil for 10 minutes over medium heat, set temperature to low heat to avoid syrup boiling. Remove from heat and let cool briefly. Press through a fine-mesh strainer or cheesecloth into a bowl. Store in a jar or bottle in the refrigerator for up to 2 weeks.
5. To make Filius Flitwick's Charmed Cherry Soda.
6. Pour a few tablespoons of cherry syrup into the bottom of 2 cocktail glasses.
7. Top up with ice.
8. Place a spoon, upside down, to the inside edge of the glass.
9. Pour in vodka (if you want).
10. Pour in soda over the spoon extremely slowly, letting it go down the side of the glass. Move the spoon upwards as it fills.
11. Garnish with a cherry, umbrella, or one of these DIY paper feather straws.

Nutrition Facts per Serving
Calories 150, Total Fat 0g, Saturated Fat 0g, Total Carbs 66g, Net Carbs 0g, PWrotein 0g, Sugar 43g, Fiber 0g, Sodium 210g, Potassium 290g

Chapter 2 Tipsy Sips From Hogwarts

Hogwarts is ladened with several magical sips and potions. From Butterbeer to pumpkin Juice, Harry Potter sure had a good time as a student as the books are packed with tales of delicious-sounding cocktails and it's no secret that most potter fans would want to order one in real life. Unfortunately, Hogwarts is a long way away from here, but we can most certainly replicate these recipes using delicious and enchanting muggle science.

Hogwarts School of Witchcraft and Wizardry is one of the best British wizarding school, located in the Scottish Highlands. It accepts magical students from Great Britain and Ireland for enrolment. It is a state-owned school funded by the Ministry of Magic. Aside from its magical affiliations, it is also home to some fantastic cocktails and potions brewed by students, potion makers and staff.

Whether you're throwing a Harry Potter party and you want to impress your friends with a variety of enchanting drinks, or you need the perfect beverage to pair with a weekend Harry Potter movie marathon, the following cocktails are classic for fans of the magical beverages from the magical Hogwarts world. Although the school's motto is Draco Dromions Nunquam Titillandus (Draco Dormiens Nvnqvam Titillandvs), which, translated from Latin, means "Never tickle a sleeping dragon," we can't promise not to try out some enchanting cocktails.

Buttered Fire Whiskey

Hello Hamorah! For the love of all things butterscotch and flamy, this enchanting potion was culled off from numerous butterbeer inspired recipes off the Harry Potter book. Everyone knows butterbeer is one of the most versatile ingredients in making most Hogwarts snacks, sweets, meals, and cakes; hence, why not a cocktail as well? This particular recipe, however, is strictly for wizards aged twenty-one and above; this is because the cocktail uses flammable Bacardi 151 to create a floating flame; we don't want the young wizards burning themselves. Special care must be taken while making this cocktail to avoid accidents.

The Fire Whisky is known as a liquor that causes a burning sensation when drunk. You see why we added the age restriction. If that doesn't scream muggle cinnamon whiskey, I don't know what does. It doesn't end there, the magic comes in as the Barcardi 151 burns, it also caramelizes some of the butterscotch soda and gives it this delicious smoky flavoring.

Prep time: 15 muggle minutes
Serves: 2

Ingredients
- 4 ounces Cinnamon Whiskey
- 12 ounces Butterscotch Soda
- 1 ounce Bacardi Rum 151

Instructions
1. Before you make the drink, ensure to chill the soda and whiskey.
2. Using two heatproof glasses at room temperature, divide your cinnamon whiskey and butterscotch soda equally into the glasses.
3. Stir drink to combine. At this stage, you can proceed to serve your alcohol, or you can get on to set it on fire using the Barcardi 151.
4. To catch on fire, divide your 151 between the two glasses, by slowly layering it on top of the drinks using the back of a bar spoon.
5. Using a stick lighter, light the top of the 151 on fire, allow to burn off. This should take approximately 10 seconds. If it doesn't burn off by then, gently blow out the fire.
6. Let them drink and glassware cool before consuming; else wise, you will burn yourself.
7. It's best to serve and sip with a straw after it's been blown out and cooled.
8. Notes: this drink can be consumed without lighting it on fire. However, if you must, use a heatproof glass as the Barcardi 151 is very flammable. Do not let it burn for an extended time, use a stick lighter to light for a lower chance of burning yourself, blow out the fire before consuming, and let the glass cool before drinking.

Nutrition Facts per Serving
Calories 135, Total Fat 0g, Saturated Fat 0g,
Total Carbs 89g, Net Carbs 34g, Protein 0g,
Sugar 75g, Fiber 0g, Sodium 0g, Potassium 0g

Golden Snitch Golden Champagne Cocktail

A tiny ball that calls the shots. Every Potterhead knows what and the importance of the golden snitch. It is a small golden ball with wings, used during the Quidditch game. Any team that catches the ball automatically wins the game as well as ends the game. Harry, being a seeker, is tasked with finding the golden snitch, a task which he never failed to fulfill. The drink draws its inspiration and characteristic golden color from this golden snitch.

The spooky Golden Snitch Cocktail. Inspired by the Harry Potter series, the sparkling bubbly golden drink is a mix of sweet apple cider, whiskey, St. Germain (elderflower liquor), lemon, maple, and spices. Just as the almost invisible golden snitch is the crown jewel of the Quidditch game, the cocktail also is a delicious blend of subtle flavors in a golden mix of goodness. This incredibly simple cocktail is nothing short of heavenly. It's the perfect moody drink to serve up anytime you need a good Harry Potter cocktail.

The Golden Snitch is a perfect blend of sweet, moody, and tangy. It is delicious without giving you an overpowering effect. It is not an overly sweet cocktail and keeps things short and sweet. I hope you all enjoy this fun Harry Potter-inspired cocktail.

Prep time: 5 muggle minutes
Serves: 1

Ingredients
- ✡ Cinnamon sugar to rim glass
- ✡ 1/4 cup apple cider
- ✡ 1/2 ounces whiskey or bourbon
- ✡ 1/2 ounce elderflower liquor (St. Germain)
- ✡ Juice from 1/2 a lemon
- ✡ 1-2 teaspoons, (more or less to taste) pure maple syrup
- ✡ Dash ground cinnamon
- ✡ Dash ground ginger
- ✡ sparkling water, for topping

Instructions
1. Rim glasses with cinnamon sugar.
2. Cast in all ingredients into a cocktail shaker except for the sparkling water.
3. Add in the ice and shake up to combine.
4. Strain contents into a glass.
5. Add one ice cube to glass and top off with sparkling water.
6. Serve with a cinnamon stick.
7. Enjoy!

Nutrition Facts per Serving
Calories 198, Total Fat 0g, Saturated Fat 0g,
Total Carbs 0g, Net Carbs 0g, Protein 0g,
Sugar 0g, Fiber 0g, Sodium 0g, Potassium 0g

Gillywater Cocktail

Gillywater is a wizarding beverage that is presumably made from Gillyweed and possibly plain water. The magical drink appeared in Harry Potter and the Goblet of Fire. Rumor has it that this Gillywater recipe is related to the real gillyflower (carnation), which is seen in winemaking recipes from the 1700s and is said to taste of spice and cloves. But this fact is certain, Gillywater is related to the magical plant gillyweed which Harry Potter consumes to win the second round of the Triwizard Tournament.

According to the potter books, gillyweed is described as a pack of slimy, grey-green rat tails, capable of stimulating temporary growth of gills and webbed fingers to help a wizard survive for extended hours underwater. Muggles may never lay hands on an actual gillyweed, but this recipe is as close as they can get to the magical cocktail. This recipe starts off with an alcoholic base of gin, giving it a tonic style of cocktail- refreshing, faintly bitter with some dash of herbs and a cucumber garnish. Using mint as the ideal herb, it incorporates coconut water for a slick, pulpy saltwater taste.

Prep time: 30 minutes
Serves: 1 pitcher

Ingredients
- 2 shots Gin (or Vodka)
- 2 shots Coconut water with pulp
- Fever-tree tonic water (or another high quality tonic with quinine)
- Cucumber halved crosswise
- Mint

Instructions
1. Firstly, when selecting a cucumber, choose a long one without any wrinkles or any nasty sponge-like spots. Wash properly and cut the stems off.
2. Peel the cucumber carefully vertically - from one end to the other. Don't throw away the skin! Keep it as it could serve to decorate your drinks for additional sliminess.
3. The aim is to get long, super-thin ribbons. Continue peeling until you get to the seeds - then stop and move to the opposite side of the cucumber, repeat the action. You can throw away the seeds, or better yet - eat them! We all know how healthy cucumber is.
4. Place the sliced cucumber, mint, gin and coconut water in a large jug. Next, pour tonic water into it. Cover and place in the refrigerator for a minimum of 1 hour. The longer you infuse it, the stronger the flavor will become.
5. Pour into glasses and serve with slices of cucumber for garnish.
6. For sweetener, mix substitute tonic water with cucumber soda.

Nutrition Facts per Serving
Calories 50, Total Fat 0g, Saturated Fat 0g,
Total Carbs 0g, Net Carbs 0g, Protein 0g,
Sugar 24g, Fiber 0g, Sodium 112g,
Potassium 213g

Pumpkintini

I wouldn't pass on this for anything. Imagine a pumpkin pie in a martini glass. Yes, I know right, heavenly. Pumpkins have always been the wizard's favorite. From Halloween to scary ghosts, everything about pumpkins spells the wizarding world. In commemoration of pumpkins and their role in making most wizarding recipes exquisite, this pumpkin martini is dedicated to all cocktail lovers.

The term 'pumpkintini' got its kinky name from the combination of two words 'pumpkin' and 'martini.' The martini, in this case, is the second most important ingredient in making the cocktail and requires you to give it a hand shake in order to get a perfect mix of the pumpkin into the drink. The flavor can be likened to a cinnamon vodka and tastes just like a slice of pumpkin pie.

Serve a pitcher of this at your Harry Potter themed party, or add it to a punch bowl with some plastic spiders floating in it for a simple creepy effect. Or serve in a sugar-rimmed martini glass for a dramatically spooky sip. The possibilities are frightening!

Prep time: 5 minutes
Serves: 2

Ingredients
- 1/2 ounce cinnamon vodka (RumChata is a substitute)
- 1-ounce vanilla vodka
- 1/4 C pumpkin puree
- Cream (depending on your preference)
- Sugar for rimming cocktail glass

Instructions
1. Rim edge of a martini glass with caramel syrup or graham cracker crumbs.
2. Put all ingredients in a shaker with ice.
3. Shake (HARD! have to mix the pumpkin).
4. Pour the drink in a glass.
5. Garnish with whipped cream, sprinkles of cracker crumbs and serve immediately.

Nutrition Facts per Serving
Calories 154, Total Fat 0g, Saturated Fat 0g, Total Carbs 0g, Net Carbs 0g, Protein 0g, Sugar 76g, Fiber 0g, Sodium 0g, Potassium 0g

Patronus Punch

'Expecto Patronum' the most used spell in the Harry Potter book. A defensive charm against dementors and other foul spirits. The Patronus charm is thought to be one of the most potent spells against dark magic. In this round, we won't be casting spells of our strongest memories to ward off evil; we'll be brewing it into a cocktail.

The Patronus Punch is a bubbly, smoky, and glowing punch with an ethereal sweet taste. It is the perfect addition to any Harry Potter themed party. It tastes best when you muddle the mint onto the bottom of the large punch bowl, thus releasing its flavors. Combine the remaining ingredients in the punch bowl, stir thoroughly to combine. Remove the mint, ladle into glasses and enjoy. Ensure you focus on your happiest memory and whisper 'Expecto Patronum' silently as you peer into the smoke; see if your Patronus takes shape! (we sure hope it does)

Prep time: 30 minutes
Serves: 1 large punch bowl

Ingredients
- ✡ 1 can frounceen limeade concentrate1 liter tonic water
- ✡ 2-liter lemon-lime soda
- ✡ Fresh mint
- ✡ 1½ cup vodka
- ✡ A BLB black light

Instructions
1. Muddle (crush) the mint in the bottom of a large punch bowl to release its flavors.
2. Combine the remaining ingredients in the punch bowl, stir enough to combine.
3. Remove the mint.
4. ladle into glasses and enjoy.

Nutrition Facts per Serving
Calories 190, Total Fat 0g, Saturated Fat 0g, Total Carbs 0g, Net Carbs 0g, Protein 0g, Sugar 0g, Fiber 0g, Sodium 0g, Potassium 0g

Butterbeer

Butterbeer is the go-to Hogwarts beverage. It is loved by the trio, Harry, Ron and Hermoine. In the real scene, butterbeer is the most accessible Potter treat at any Potter event or setting. Muggles can get a cup of this goodness at the wizarding world of Harry Potter, at Universal Studios in Hollywood or Orlando.

This, without doubt, is the best homemade butterbeer you would ever taste. It rightly puts the mug in "muggle" and without a doubt is a delicious homemade butterbeer. A pure brown sugar and butter syrup get topped with cream soda and a dollop of cream in this wildly popular drink. To be very authentic with the recipe, you can use plain cream soda, caramel, and butter extract. This really adds for a more buttery flavor and brings you closer to what the real thing tastes like. For a simpler recipe, simply use the plain cream soda. This is quite yummy as well and you do not have to spend so much on extracts either. Either way, it tastes fantastic.

Prep time: 60 minutes
Serves: 4

Ingredients
- 1 cup light or dark brown sugar
- 2 tablespoons water
- 6 tablespoons butter
- ½ teaspoon salt
- ½ teaspoon cider vinegar
- ¾ cup heavy cream, divided
- ½ teaspoon rum extract
- 4 (12 ounces) bottle cream soda

Instructions
1. Cast ingredients in a small saucepan over medium heat, combine the brown sugar and water. Bring to a gentle boil and cook, often stirring, until the mixture reads 240°F on a candy thermometer.
2. Cast in the salt, butter, vinegar, and ¼ portions of heavy cream. Set down to cool to room temperature.
3. Stir in rum extract once the mixture has cooled.
4. In a medium bowl, combine 2 tablespoons of the brown sugar mixture and the rest parts of about 1/2 cup of heavy cream.
5. Use an electric mixer to whisk until just thickened, but not thoroughly whipped, about 2 to 3 minutes.
6. To serve: divide the brown sugar mixture between 4 tall glasses (about 1/4 cup for each glass). Add 1/4 cup of cream soda to each glass, then stir to combine.
7. Fill each glass nearly to the top with additional cream soda, then spoon the whipped topping over each.

Nutrition Facts per Serving
Calories 146, Total Fat 76g, Saturated Fat 0g,
Total Carbs 50g, Net Carbs 0g, Protein 12g,
Sugar 25g, Fiber 0g, Sodium 0g, Potassium 0g

Firewhisky

Firewhisky is an alcoholic drink consumed mostly by powerful wizards and witches. Unfortunately, those under the age of seventeen are not allowed to buy it, implying that they may not be allowed to drink it. This rule is not always followed. Popular brands include Ogden's Old Firewhisky and Blishen's Firewhisky. It is known to cause a burning sensation when drunk, and for filling one's body with courage.

"The firewhisky seared Harry's throat. It seemed to burn feeling back into him, dispelling the numbness and sense of unreality and firing him with something that was like courage. "

—The effect firewhisky has

You've read the recipes for butterbeer - but have you ever wondered what firewhiskey tasted like? Well, it's a lot like if you were to snog Norbert the Norwegian Ridgeback (I can imagine), but don't take my word for it! Ron Weasley confessed to almost purchasing a glass of firewhiskey at Hog's Head during the Dumbledore's Army meeting. Hermione was angered at that, furiously reminding him of his prefect status. He instead had Butterbeer. Predominantly cast in Harry Potter and the Cursed Child, firewhisky fills the drinker with courage and causes a burning sensation when drunk.

Prep time: 1 hour 5 minutes
Serves: 2

Ingredients
- 250 ml Whiskey (Old Dan Tucker Kentucky Bourbon Whiskey is recommended.)
- 2 cinnamon sticks
- 1/8 cup brown sugar
- 2 tablespoon Tabasco sauce

Instructions
1. Pour as much whiskey as you like into a cup or shot glass.
2. Combine the sugar, cinnamon sticks and whiskey and allow to sit in a sealed bottle for a while, let's say 1 hour.
3. Mix the tabasco sauce into a glass of the whiskey, serve and enjoy.

Nutrition Facts per Serving
Calories 120, Total Fat 0g, Saturated Fat 0g, Total Carbs 0g, Net Carbs 0g, Protein 0g, Sugar 50g, Fiber 0g, Sodium 312g, Potassium 112g

The Mudblood Cocktail

"filthy little Mudblood" how painfully that stung Hermionee's heart when Malfoy referred to her as one. The name Mudblood is taken from Harry Potter, which is the worst name one can call another in that world. Poor Hermoine Granger cried out her eyes when Draco Malfoy referred to her as one, thus taunting her for her non-magical origins. Lineage has been a constant issue in the Harry Potter world. Malfoy is priding his pureblood lineage while Hermione is showing that it doesn't matter your parentage, a great wizard is made not born.

Since we can't all run down to The Leaky Cauldron every night, let's take a look at how to make a scintillating glass in honor of our devoted muggle. Though she was trying at times, where would Harry be without his good friend, Hermione, with her extreme intelligence and book smarts and caring heart? In honor of our brave heroine.

This combination of Midori, Grenadine, and orange juice, is served chilled over ice in a rocks glass. After one of these, you will be feeling as proud as Hermione to be a Mudblood.

Prep time: 5 minutes
Serves: 2

Ingredients
- 30 ml orange juice
- 30 ml Midori
- Dash Grenadine
- 30 ml Pimm's No. 1
- 15 ml spiced rum

Instructions
1. Pour all ingredients except grenadine into a shaker with ice.
2. Shake well then strain into a chilled lowball glass with ice.
3. add a splash of grenadine, which will sink to the bottom.
4. Serve. Stir to enjoy.

Nutrition Facts per Serving
Calories 191, Total Fat 0g, Saturated Fat 0g, Total Carbs 54g, Net Carbs 0g, Protein 0g, Sugar 54g, Fiber 0g, Sodium 3.22g, Potassium 51g

Pureblood

Pureblood is the ideal cocktail for powerful witches and wizards whose bloodline is as pure as crystal without the infiltration of muggles. Malfoy may have been out of line when he called Hermoine a Mudblood, but let's face it, the wizarding world is run and governed by purebloods. This sip is inspired by the raw, undiluted ancestry of pureblood wizards. Only powerful muggles, capable of withstanding its intoxicating grip should dare to try it, else, stick to the good old Mudblood cocktail.

The Pureblood cocktail is a strong one, with the Vodka taking a huge part in that. To capture the true cruel essence of most pureblood wizards, a sweet and sour mix is incorporated into the cocktail. Of course, we didn't forget some muggles may want to take a sip, hence the raspberry liqueur and raspberry garnish. One thing for sure, this is made by and for powerful purebloods.

Prep time: 5 minutes
Serves: 2

Ingredients
- 2½ ounces vodka
- 4 ounces sweet and sour mix
- 1 ounce raspberry liqueur
- Raspberry garnish

Instructions
1. Add vodka, sweet and sour mix, and raspberry liqueur to a shaker with ice.
2. Shake to chill
3. Pour into a shot glass.
4. Garnish with raspberry.

Nutrition Facts per Serving
Calories 114, Total Fat 0g, Saturated Fat 0g, Total Carbs 0g, Net Carbs 0g, Protein 0g, Sugar 43g, Fiber 0g, Sodium 0g, Potassium 0g

Golden Shimmery Bubbly Mocktail

Just a casual sip for the perfect evening. The Golden Shimmery Bubbly Mocktails are one of the golden snitches inspired Harry Potter cocktails. The shimmery effect gives it the much desired magical impact of the golden snitch. You can't blame crafty muggles for trying to pimp things up with this one. Initially, when created, the Mocktail was Rose Gold in color, slightly softer than copper and pinker than regular gold. However, with time, the recipe was corrected and perfected and with that stood right to its name.

The shimmery mocktail is simply an easy elderflower champagne cocktail with a touch of magical gold luster dust. Edible, of course, and mesmerizingly beautiful. To keep things simple and easy, it is non-alcoholic, which means everyone can take a sip!

Prep time: 30 minutes
Serves: 4

Ingredients
- 4.5 fl ounces elderflower liqueur
- 2/3 cups Sparkling Grape Juice
- 4¾ teaspoons gold luster dust

Instructions
1. To prepare ahead of time for this gold shimmery champagne cocktail, pour a portion of the elderflower liqueur (or the homemade cheat's St-Germain liqueur) into a bottle (roughly the amount you'll think you need, you can always make more).
2. Add enough gold luster dust to the elderflower liqueur base and mix to make it shimmer.
3. Shake up content thoroughly in a cocktail shaker.
4. Add sparkling grape juice or apple juice depending on preference.
5. Serve chilled.

Nutrition Facts per Serving
Calories 80, Total Fat 0g, Saturated Fat 0g, Total Carbs 0g, Net Carbs 0g, Protein 0g, Sugar 0g, Fiber 0g, Sodium 0g, Potassium 0g

Goblet of Fire

The original goblet of fire was brought out to choose which person from each school would compete in the Triwizard Tournament. In the book, one sip bound the chosen challenger to a binding contract. This version is so delicious you'll be 'bound' to nothing more than finishing the glass. The cocktail is created for and by adults who enjoy magical twists to their cocktail glass. With its little sparks and flames, it'll surely ignite your desires on fire.

Just like everything Harry Potter inspired, the delicious cocktail comes with an intoxicating touch of alcohol. It was created to channel the essence of the actual goblet of fire from the good old potter books. With a subtle combination of sweet fruit and coffee, it's even better when you top it off with a touch of cream. To finish it off, it comes with a dash of overproof rum. Let's not forget the flame (lower proof rums will not burn as quickly). As with all flaming cocktails, take caution: extinguish the fire properly and don't allow anyone who's had one too many near the lit glass. Take absolute discretion, put on a magic show for your guests, and enjoy.

Prep time: 15 minutes
Serves: 4 sips

Ingredients
- 2 ounces Ty Ku Liqueur
- 1-ounce coffee liqueur (Kahlua)
- 1 teaspoon cream
- 1-ounce 151-proof rum
- Dash cinnamon (grated)

Instructions
1. Get all ingredients ready.
2. Fill up ice, cast in two liqueurs in a cocktail shaker and shake very well.
3. Strain contents into a wine goblet or cocktail glass.
4. Pour in cream slowly, to make it float on top of the glass with a spoon.
5. Float the rum on top of the cream using a similar technique.
6. Light up the rum using a match.
7. Sprinkle cinnamon on the flame as it burns.
8. Put out the flames with a hand wave and give the drink a slow stir.
9. Voila! Serve and enjoy.

Notes:
Always use thick glassware so the heat of the flame doesn't crack the glass. Don't let it burn long, either. Even the thickest glass won't stand up to prolonged heat.

Nutrition Facts per Serving
Calories 0, Total Fat 0g, Saturated Fat 0g, Total Carbs 0g, Net Carbs 0g, Protein 0g, Sugar 0g, Fiber 0g, Sodium 0g, Potassium 0

Chapter 3 Beast Inspired Sips

The beasts inspired sips are culled from famous magical creatures featured in the Harry Potter books. The Fantastic Beasts: Crimes of Grindelwald is the sequel to the Harry Potter books and embodies the essence of beasts we've come to love in the books. Mystical animals such as werewolves and phoenixes were brought to life in the Harry Potter books. But in the chapter, an exclusive cocktail is created to represent the exact characteristics of the beasts.

These beasts inspired sips are a set of entirely enchanting concoction. An intoxicating combination of flavors from Spiced Rum, Triple Sec, Blue Curaçao, and orange, these cocktails will tease your taste buds in all the right ways. Add in a little crushed dry ice and these Beastly Cocktails look every bit as magical as its name implies. And just like magic, these cocktails are delicious and a little dangerous, so fly with caution!

Fizzing Whizbees Levitator

It has always been everyone's dream to fly, even if it means floating a few inches off the ground. You would give anything to make that dream come true, right? Well, you won't need to give much; just a glass of the Fizzing Whizbees Levitator is all you need. The Queenbee's exquisite recipe will make anyone who takes as much as a shot of the cocktail to float off the ground.

As unbelievable as it sounds, the Hogsmeade faithful would argue that there is no liquor as levitating as the fizzing whizbees. Hogsmeade might be in wonderland, but our recipe is just a foot away from where you are and, as such, it shouldn't be a big deal to levitate with a chilled glass of whizbees.

So why not tag along as we celebrate our innate wizard and levitate together with our appetizing cocktail made from pop rocks, Zotz candy, and of course, a splash of bourbon?

Prep time: 5 minutes
Cook time: 10 minutes
Total time: 15 minutes
Serves: 1 cocktail

Ingredients
- ½ cup bourbon (or any liquor of your choice)
- ½ cup simple syrup
- ¼ cup Campari
- ⅛ cup lemon juice
- 1 large egg white
- 1 mug of ginger ale
- 1 crushed Zotz candy
- 1 packet pop rocks candy
- Ice cubes

Instructions
1. Make the simple syrup by mixing sugar into boiling water and stirring for 10 minutes.
2. Mix the bourbon and simple syrup together with the Campari and lemon juice into a large pitcher and set aside.
3. Add the pop rocks into a shaker with the egg white, ginger ale, and shake well.
4. Combine the bourbon mixture into the shaker and shake vigorously.
5. Pour into a glass with ice and top cocktail with Zotz candy.

Nutrition Facts per Serving
Calories 190kcal, Total Fat 7g, Saturated Fat 6g,
Total Carbs 32g, Net Carbs 0g, Protein 1g,
Sugar 31g, Fiber 0g, Sodium 10mg, Potassium 0g

Hair of the Three-Headed Dog (Cerberus)

Ever heard of the saying... 'The hair of the dog that bit you soothes the pain?' Where better to get dog hair than a three-headed dog? Fluffy was an enormous male three-headed dog that was tendered to by Hagrid. But the interesting fact here is that it was unable to withstand falling asleep when he hears the sound of music.

The Hair Of The Three-Headed Dog cocktail does the same for you amidst your period of head-splitting worries. And with it, you're sure to resist the effects of that hangover. Do you know a better Halloween party drink?

Just like the moment, you feel like having everything under control, this cocktail just like Fluffy puts up a hedge around you in your most unguarded hour, and with its soothing effect ensures that you can't resist a good rest time. But this time you wouldn't need the weird beast snarling around you. No, just a well-brewed glass of this Michelada mutt.

You may have heard that it takes months to brew a perfect cocktail in the JK Rowling series. And that maybe you'll need some irregular metal urn that emits spiral fumes, coupled with a wand, just to produce a glass of this potion.

Not to worry though, because if they got theirs in months, I'll show you how to get yours in minutes. Let's see.

Prep time: 10 minutes
Cook time: 10 minutes
Total time: 20 minutes
Serves: 1

Ingredients
- ¼ cup tequila
- ½ cup tomato juice
- 1 tablespoon lime juice
- 1 tablespoon English sauce
- ½ tablespoon Tabasco sauce
- 1½ cup Modelo
- 2 tablespoons Kosher salt
- ¼ tablespoon chili powder
- 1 stalk well-trimmed root celery
- Ice cubes

Instructions
1. Combine the juices and sauces in a big mug. Mix the tomato juice, tequila, English and Tabasco sauces in the mug, stir well and set aside.
2. Mix the Kosher salt and chili powder together in a little bowl for the running of the cocktail glass.
3. Rim the glass with salt and chili powder. Dip the rim of the glass into a slice of lime to get it moist, then roll the outer parts in the mixture of salt and chilli powder to coat it.
4. Get the well-trimmed root celery and grate it to size.
5. Fill the glass with ice cubes up to half of the glass.
6. Then pour the juice and sauce mixture from the mug and stir well.
7. Serve with a little beer (modela) topping (optional) and garnish with the grated celery.

Nutrition Facts per Serving
Calories 502 kcal, Total Fat 1g, Saturated Fat 0g, Total Carbs 13g, Net Carbs 0g, Protein 2g, Sugar 6g, Fiber 0g, Sodium 24mg, Potassium 31mg

Phoenix Feather

We all know the Phoenix is an adorable bird and its feather twice as adorable as it is powerful. The warmness that comes from its councey feathers could put the wildest boar to a sound sleep. Who knows if it's where the cocktail got its drowsing effect?

This rare brew mixture of a drink has the ability to soothe a fiery nerve after a disturbing experience and also cure the worst cases of insomnia. The Phoenix feather original cocktail comes in handy after a stressful workday to induce its relaxing effects.

Ollivander and Dumbledore knew the power of phoenix feathers. Even though they had other motives aside from ours, it still goes to show the uniqueness of one of the rarest items on the planet.

After much experimentation and research, I have concluded that only three substances could create such a calming effect, chief amongst which is the Phoenix feather.

Ollivander describing the Phoenix feather

Ollivander might need to get to the ends of the earth to get a phoenix feather, but you? Nada! Our recipe here gives you endless access to an unforgettable experience of the Phoenix Feather cocktail.

Prep time: 5 minutes
Serves: 2 serves

Ingredients
- ½ cup Remy Martin
- ¼ cup sweet vermouth
- ½ cup Campari
- ⅛ cup Benedictine
- 2 tablespoons Regan's orange bitters
- 1 slice grapefruit
- Ice cubes

Instructions
1. Mix the Remy Martin, sweet vermouth, Campari, and Benedictine into a mug and stir well
2. Add Regan's orange bitters to the mixture.
3. Then blend the slice of grapefruit to extract its juice.
4. Combine all the liquor in a cocktail shaker and shake well.
5. Strain into a glass filled to the half with some ice cubes and serve.

Nutrition Facts per Serving
Calories 180kcal, Total Fat 0g, Saturated Fat 0g,
Total Carbs 28g, Net Carbs 0g, Protein 0g,
Sugar 7g, Fiber 0g, Sodium 0.13g, Potassium 0.23g

The Bloody Baron Caesar

The Bloody Baron Caesar is a fantastic drink to start or end an amazing brunch or party time. While some may argue that the Bloody Mary has a superior vibe, there are numerous reasons why I'll beg to disagree. Most notable among them is the chief ingredient used in the making of this unique cocktail.

Its calming effect has the capacity to ignite the same love that was flickered in the heart of the bloody baron. So strong will it be that there won't be a reason to show the temper that characterized the Bloody Baron in Harry Potter and the Philosopher's stone.

for the baron was a hot-tempered man

Helen Ravenclaw on the Baron; Harry Potter and the Philosopher's Stone

The Clamato juice is the main ingredient used to make the Bloody Caesar as opposed to the tomato juice used in the Bloody Mary's. But Clamato, as we know, is a blend of the tomato and clam juices. Awesome, isn't it? That's why I'll always say the Bloody Mary has nothing on the Bloody Caesar! On its own, I'll recommend the Clamato juice any day.

Now combine it with the contents of our recipe and you are in for wonderful cocktail blend. Below are some of the basic ingredients you need to get yourself a Bloody glass of Caesar. You could add your preferred variety (some people prefer rum or tequila to vodka) or any other you deem fit. The more the merrier!

Prep time: 5 minutes
Serves: 2

Ingredients
- ½ cup Vodka (or your preferred drink - rum, tequila, or brandy)
- 2 tablespoons celery salt
- 1 slice a quartered lime
- 3 cups Clamato juice
- 2 teaspoons English sauce
- 1 teaspoon hot sauce
- ½ teaspoon freshly ground paper
- 1 teaspoon well-grated horseradish
- Ice cubes

Instructions
1. Put the two tablespoons of celery salt in a small dish or shallow bowl for the running of the glass.
2. Moisten the rims of the glass with the slice of lime and dip into the bowl of celery salt. Roll the glass to coat the rim with the salt and shake off the excesses.
3. Mix the lime juice and Clamato juice in a hug and stir well.
4. Add the English sauce, hot sauce, grated horseradish and leftover celery salt in another mug with the vodka.
5. Combine the vodka mixture and juice mixture into the same pitcher and stir.
6. Pour into a glass with ice cubes.

Nutrition Facts per Serving
Calories 265, Total Fat 2g, Saturated Fat 0g,
Total Carbs 24g, Net Carbs 0g, Protein 0g,
Sugar 8g, Fiber 0g, Sodium 15mg, Potassium 0g

Happy Elf Cocktail

Harry knows too well the benefits of keeping Dobby happy because no matter how annoying he can be, a happy elf means a plethora of good tidings. Happy elf cocktail promises happiness in the magnitude of Dobby's ecstasy when he was freed from the Malfoys.

The Happy Elf Cocktail drink is an outstanding brunch time drink that restores your energy and enthusiasm after being exhausted from the morning rush. The glow on Dobby's face whenever he gets a gift of a sock has nothing on the excitement that comes with the happy elf cocktail drink.

If you want a drink to light up your guests and shake them up this holiday, you just found yourself a simple quick but perfect cocktail drink. What better drink to start off your festive party than an elf inspired fun drink?

Elves are adorable creatures, and with the type of help they render to their masters, they deserve to be kept happy. Who says only Santa could get a treat on Christmas Eve? Our favorite toymakers (elves) deserve to be treated to an amazing mixture, too.

So, Santa could keep on with his milk and cookies. We can make this cocktail with the ever-willing help elves.

Prep time: 10 minutes
Serves: 4

Ingredients
- ½ cup vodka (rum or tequila can also come in handy)
- ¼ cup white cranberry juice
- 3 tablespoons freshly ground maraschino cherries
- ¼ cup melon liquor (any beer can stand in for Michelada)
- Ice cubes
- ¼ teaspoon celery salt for rimming

Instructions
1. Put the salt in a shallow bowl. Then moisten the rim of the serving glass and dip into the bowl of celery salt. Shake off excesses and allow them to dry.
2. Mix the vodka and cranberry juice in a mug. Add the maraschino cherries to garnish.
3. Top off with the melon liqueur or beer.
4. Pour into a rimmed glass with ice cubes. Serve chilled.

Nutrition Facts per Serving
Calories 170kcal, Total Fat 0g, Saturated Fat 0g,
Total Carbs 32g, Net Carbs 0g, Protein 0g,
Sugar 8g, Fiber 0g, Sodium 24mg, Potassium 43mg.

Unicorn Blood Cocktail

Just like we were told by JK Rowling in the Harry Potter series, the unicorn blood gives you a breath of life even at the point of exhaustion. But to get unicorn blood these days is like getting the devil's balls. I'm not sure there's a more impossible task. Nonetheless, we have in this drink the same rejuvenating prowess that makes Voldemort stand out.

The Unicorn Blood Cocktail comes with the ignition power that resurrects a dying soul. What better drink to spice up your Halloween than the sacred source of Voldemort's power? But not worry, it isn't that scary because unlike Quirrell we won't have to kill any unicorns.

Instead, we'll chop up some raspberries and peaches as we perform our own little but bloodless magic. That also frees us from the curse that comes with drinking the unicorn's blood.

Instead, with a blend of raspberry and peach, we have made a drink that will rival Voldemort's power potion anytime. So, come along, let's rekindle your inner Voldemort with our Unicorn Blood Cocktail.

Prep time: 10 minutes
Serves: 3 drinks

Ingredients
- 1 cup raspberry juice
- ½ cup peach blend
- ½ tablespoon icing sugar to taste
- ¼ cup water
- Shimmering liqueur (A pinch of gold dust and ¼ cup Vodka)
- A pinch of purple petal dust (to give the enticing purple color to the drink)
- Ice cubes

Instructions
1. Pulverize the raspberries by either soft blending or meshing in a sieve to also remove the seeds.
2. Mix the icing sugar into the raspberry little by little until it gets to your desired taste and keep in the fridge to chill.
3. Mix the vodka with the purple petal dust to make the shimmering liquid. Also, add the gold dust if you wish.
4. Line the wall as of the moist glass with the purple petal dust and add some ice cubes to the glass.
5. Pour the vodka mix into the purple glasses and leave it half-filled. Then add the pulverized raspberry to fill up the glass.
6. Serve the unicorn blood cocktail chilled.

Nutrition Facts per Serving
Calories 200kcal, Total Fat 0g, Saturated Fat 0g, Total Carbs 49g, Net Carbs 0g, Protein 1g, Sugar 46g, Fiber 0g, Sodium 49mg, Potassium 52mg

Chapter 4 Potions of Enchantment

Potions of enchantment are special potions aimed at altering the natural cause of events, nature and emotions. They are brewed to alter one's natural way of behavior. Potions are magical liquids which give either a positive or negative effect for a period of time. There are various types of enchanting potions, those brewed and aimed at effecting everything they hit and those brewed and thrown as charms at a target.

Enchantments are like magical armors, weapons and tools of special abilities. To enchant a target requires maximum experience levels gained by mining the power of creating some special potion. Brewing is the method to create both types of potions and this chapter goes into detail to discuss special enchanting potions from the Harry Potter books.

Black Magic

If you love the Harry Potter books so much as to crave its metaphysical atmosphere, then the black magic cocktail is the drink for you. The Black Magic cocktail is a sinister, shimmering fluid that is deceptively sweet and made with fruity beverages, black vodka, orange juice, and cherry juice. There are different shades of the drink stemming from your choice of ingredients.

There are numerous inconsistencies in the color variation of the different shades of this cocktail drink. Sometimes the drink is black, which is the original color from the Hogwarts cherry color, and sometimes it's red. The choice of the cherry brand is the major reason for this variation.

But to proffer a lasting solution to these issues, some companies have produced black vodka for reasons like this. However, most people find it difficult to locate these vodkas in shops and so resort to making one as an improvised black martini. But the process is a bit messy and might stain the lips as most food dyes do.

That won't be your problem though; with this recipe, you'll have your Black Magic cocktail with a swivel of your wand. Now that will make me Harry and you Hermione. Come with me, let's go mix some lime martini and daiquiri.

Prep time: 2 minutes 30 seconds
Cook time 2 minutes 30 seconds
Total time 5mins
Serves: 1

Ingredients
- ¼ cup black vodka
- ½ cup lime juice
- ½ cup simple syrup
- ¼ cup black currant (optional if you wish for a non-alcoholic drink)
- Ice cubes
- Pearl dust
- ½ cup cherry juice
- ½ cup orange juice
- 1 cup maraschino cherry syrup

Instructions
1. Pour the black vodka and lime juice into a cocktail shaker (you use black currant in place of the vodka for non-alcoholic mixture). Then shake the mixture vigorously.
2. Into a separate mug add enough pearl dust to make it shimmering, then add on the ice until it gets to the liquid line.
3. Add the cherry juice, orange juice, and simple syrup to the cocktail shaker and shake well.
4. Then empty the contents of the cocktail shaker into the mug and stir with a bar spoon for about 10 seconds until the cocktail is chilled.
5. Strain into a martini glass and top off with the orange peels and maraschino cherries as you wish.

Nutrition Facts per Serving
Calories 272kcal, Total Fat 0g, Saturated Fat 0g,
Total Carbs 16.62g, Net Carbs 4.88g, Protein 0.75g,
Sugar 8g, Fiber 0g, Sodium 23mg, Potassium 42mg

Amortencia

Amortencia is the most powerful love potion in existence. It causes a powerful infatuation or obsession from the drinker. It has a distinctive mother-of-pearl sheen, and steam rises from it in characteristic spirals.

Rightly described as the most effective love potion in the Harry Potter series, Amortencia is popular for its mother-of-pearl radiance. Remarkable about it also is the spiraling fog that emanates from it and of course the different aromas it gives whoever that smells it. A treacle tart broomstick smell for Harry, fresh-cut grass for Hermione and a flowery smell to Ginny Weasley; the potion gives each person a smell of something they find most attractive.

...a gold-colored cauldron that was emitting one of the most seductive scents Harry had ever inhaled: somehow it reminded him of treacle tart, the smell of broomstick handle and something he might have smelled at the burrow.

Harry Potter and the Half-blood Prince

"They chose the one nearest a gold-coloured cauldron that was emitting one of the most seductive scents Harry had ever inhaled: somehow it reminded him simultaneously of treacle tart, the woody smell of a broomstick handle, and something flowery he thought he might have smelled at the Burrow. He found that he was breathing very slowly and deeply and that the potion's fumes seemed to be filling him up like drink."

—The aroma as smelled by Harry Potter

Amortencia doesn't create love but a momentary false feeling of affection which wears out if the victim stops taking the potion. The impact is immediate, with the victim becoming pale and unnecessarily passionate towards others. It's a perfect cocktail to serve up for Valentine's Day and other special occasions.

Prep time: 10 minutes
Serves: 1 drink (potent for 24 hourrs)

Ingredients
- 1 pint fresh red raspberry
- 1 cup fresh pomegranates
- 2 ounces pomegranate juice
- ½ ounce grenadine
- 1 cup vodka
- ¼ tablespoon pearl dust
- Ice cubes

Instructions
1. Blend the fresh pomegranates and mix the liquid with the pomegranate juice.
2. Get a cocktail shaker and add the pomegranate mixture together with the vodka, grenadine, and ice.
3. Shake the mixture vigorously for 30 seconds.
4. Pour into a glass and stir with the pearl dust (don't mix pearl dust before shaking so that it doesn't stick to the shaker).
5. Sprinkle the raspberries on top. You could use red soda in place of vodka if the kids would have some of it.

Nutrition Facts per Serving
Calories 64 Kcal, carbs 8g, total carbs 10g, total fat 0g, potassium 21mg, total sugar 6g, Vitamin C 2.6mg, fiber 0 mg, protein 0 mg.

Felix Felicia

In need of a bit of luck for your day? Then a pint of Felix Felicis is all you are required to gulp. Known as Liquid Luck, the potion transforms your regular day to be an incredible one. It gives the drinker a huge chunk of luck during its potency period. Yes, you gulp down a pint and you're good to go for that interview or proposal presentation.

Good fortune may be a scarce product to come across, but not if you have an ace portioner, Zygmunt. Liquid luck ensures that your fate gets a quick fix and lines up the choicest opportunities and lightens up your day.

"Mine own invention, my masterpiece; the crowning achievement of my career. Bottled good fortune; Brewed correctly. The drinker of this potion will be lucky in all their endeavors, but be warned... Excessive consumption is highly toxic and can cause extreme recklessness. "

Zygmunt Budge; Wonder Book of Potions

Harry Potter won a small vial of Felix Felicia from Professor Slughorn for brewing the best Draught of Living Death potion in the class (using the instructions of Severus Snape's textbook). The bottle would give Harry Potter twelve hour's worth of effects.

"Trust me, I know what I'm doing... or at least, Felix does."

—Harry Potter after drinking Felix Felicia

Horace Slughorn claimed that he used the potion twice in his life: once when he was 24 years old, and again when he was 57, each resulting in a perfect day.

Great care should be taken when using the liquid luck potion so as not to take in excess quantities as the effects are kind of grave. Felix Felicia possibly works by providing the drinker with the best possible scenario. This usually registers in the drinker's mind in the form of an unusual urge to take a certain action, or as a voice telling him to do so. Whenever you spot signs of giddiness and reckless display of overconfidence from an individual, look out he must have doted on Felix Felicia. That said, you should also be alert when preparing the potion as it poses like dangers of overdose when formulated wrongly.

Zygmunt might not be here with his shoulder eggs and squill bulb, but we'll show you a potent way of preparing a jar of Liquid of Luck. And never forget what Hermoine told Harry,

"Luck can only get you so far, Harry... Luck is not powerful enough to get through a powerful incantation."

Hermione explaining to Harry Potter the limits of luck induced by the potion

Prep time: 8 minutes
Chill time: 1 hour
Serves: 6

Ingredients
- Sweet and gold crystals for hemming the glass
- 1 teaspoon ginger freshly ground
- ¼ teaspoon freshly ground turmeric
- ¼ cup ice crushed
- 1 peeled Clementine
- 2 cups lemonade
- 1 cup pineapple juice
- 1½ cup vodka (if you want it to be alcoholic)
- ¼ cup lemon-lime soda (for the non-alcoholic version)
- ½ cup simple syrup (to be used in the alcoholic version)

For the simple syrup
- 1 cup of sugar
- 1 cup of water

Instructions
1. For starters, prepare the simple syrup if you'll by mixing the sugar and water in boiling water and boil for 10 minutes and allow to chill.
2. Then rim the glass with gold crystals by dipping the wet rim of the glass into a shallow bowl of gold crystals. Turn the glass in a circular manner to enhance adhesion.
3. Blend the Clementine and pour out in a large mixing bowl.
4. Then add all other ingredients, the juices, ginger, and turmeric into the large mixing bowl and stir properly.
5. Then pour back in the blender with the crushed ice, simple syrup and Vodka (or the soda) and blend together.
6. Pour out to the rimmed glass and serve.

Nutrition Facts per Serving
Calories 80 Kcal, Total Fat 0g, Saturated Fat 0g,
Total Carbs 162mg, Net Carbs 0.16g, Protein 0g,
Sugar 7g, Fiber 0g, Sodium 24 mg, Potassium 2.3g.

Wolfsbane

Most times our cute dogs tend to exhibit a wolf characteristic. Who knows, it might be undergoing lycanthropy and the symptoms are best imagined. When such signs are detected a pint of the Wolfsbane potion could work magic in soothing the effects. Severus Snape brewed this potion for Remus Lupin during Lupin's year as Defence Against the Dark Arts professor at Hogwarts School of Witchcraft and Wizardry. Harry thought Severus Snape was poisoning Remus Lupin and later told his friends about it after they came back from Honeydukes.

Despite its blue smoke emissions and unsavory taste, the Wolfsbane relieves the symptoms of lycanthropy but doesn't prefer curative solutions to it. Since Aconite (or monkshood, a very poisonous material) is the major ingredient used in making Wolfsbane, it's wise to stick with the recommended prescription.

This is necessary to maintain its calming effect on the drinker and not transcend to more dangerous effects. The gobletful per day prescription at full moon should be religiously adhered to and is necessary to keep the werewolf in check, at least for the period of transformation.

It was incredibly tough to prepare as suggested by Slughorn that Damocles put in extreme efforts to make it. Also, the processes are erratic, given that Aconite is a hazardous substance it could cause harm if prepared the wrong way.

No need for worries. We listed an elaborate step-by-step guide on how to make an effective wolfsbane potion.

Prep time: 5 minutes
Cook time: 5 minutes
Serves: 2

Ingredients
- ½ cup Fernet Branca cola
- ½ cup vodka (alcoholic mixture)
- ¼ cup red soda (for non-alcoholic mixture)
- ¼ teaspoon finely ground monkshood
- ½ cup water
- 1 cup lemon-lime soda

Instructions
1. Dissolve the finely ground monkshood in water and stir to mix properly.
2. Mix the vodka and lemon line soda in another mug. Add the red soda in place of the vodka if you don't want an alcoholic potion.
3. Add the monkshood mixture and the soda mix in a cocktail shaker and shake vigorously.
4. Pour out in a glass and add the Fernet Branca cola to enhance the taste.
5. Nutritional facts per serving

Nutrition Facts per Serving
Calories 63 kcal, Total Fat 1.25mg,
Saturated Fat 0g, Total Carbs 6g,
Net Carbs 6g, Protein 0g, Sugar 5g,
Fiber 0g, Sodium 0.67g, Potassium 0.46g

Polyjuice Potion

Have you ever wished to be another person? Say you just want to look different from your normal self for just a little period of time? Then the Polyjuice Potion is your one time chance. Polyjuice Potion allows you to assume the appearance of someone else.

The Polyjuice Potion, which is a complex and time-consuming concoction, is best left to highly skilled witches and wizards. The fact that Hermione is able to make a competent Polyjuice Potion at the age of twelve is testimony to her outstanding magical ability, because it is a potion that many adult witches and wizards fear to attempt.

"Polyjuice Potion has the power to transform the drinker into somebody else. The recipe can be found in Moste Potente Potions, which is housed in the Restricted Section of the Hogwarts library. It is a very complicated potion and requires ingredients such as lacewing flies, leeches, fluxweed, knotgrass, powdered horn of a Bicorn and shredded skin of a Boomslang as well as a bit of whoever the drinker intends to turn into. Harry, Ron and Hermione want to take the potion so that they can turn into Slytherins and find out if Draco Malfoy is the heir of Slytherin, as they suspect."

Harry Potter and the Half-Blood Prince

In Harry's world, the difficult and formidable potion requires about a month of meticulous processes to prepare. Its highly advanced 2-stage preparation is always a heinous task for any witch or wizard who wishes to embark.

While it can be used to alter age and gender, the Polyjuice Potion can be used only for human to human transformation. You can't use it to transform an animal or half-human to a human being.

The recipe can be found in Moste Potente Potions which is domiciled at the restricted section of the Hogwarts library. It is a very complicated potion and requires ingredients like lacewig flies, leeches, fluxweed, and knotgrass, powdered horn of a Bicorn and shredded skin of Boomslang.

Harry Potter and the Goblet of Fire

The real ingredients are kind of scary and repulsive, most especially the part that requires any piece of the person you want to be. Scary isn't it? Like you'll get the hair strand or nail clips of your neighbor who lives next door that you wish to look like.

Not to worry, I will show you how to make the non-scary version of the Polyjuice Potion.

Prep time: 3 muggle minutes
Cook time: 5 minutes
Total time: 10 minutes
Serves: 6 potions

Ingredients

- 1 cup kiwi juice
- 8 ounces apple juice
- 2 cups sprite
- 3 cups lime sherbet
- 3-4 dips food coloring (green or turquoise)
- Whipped cream

Instructions

1. Put the lime sherbet into a bowl and pep with a fork to crush into smaller pieces.
2. Then gently pour the sprite into the bowl. You should be alert to avoid the foaming overreaction and allow the foam to settle.
3. Then empty the cup of kiwi juice into the bowl and stir well.
4. Add the remaining Ingredients in a mug including the coloring until it's green to taste and stir vigorously to mix.
5. Then pour the two different juice mixes into a cocktail shaker and shake well.
6. You can top with the whipped cream if you wish.
7. Serve chilled in goblets.

Nutrition Facts per Serving

Calories 165 Kcal, Total Fat 0g, Saturated Fat 0g, Total Carbs 39g, Net Carbs 39g, Protein 0g, Sugar 35g, Fiber 0g, Sodium 44mg, Potassium 47mg, calcium 33mg, iron 9.3mg.

Lightning Source UK Ltd.
Milton Keynes UK
UKHW021441160321
380432UK00001B/38